easy Foam Crafts

Colorful stickers and easy-cut sheets make these projects super-fun for kids!

LEISURE ARTS, INC. • Little Rock, Arkansas

AF798557

Puppet Theatre

SHOPPING LIST

- ☐ 14" X 22" mini corrugated tri-fold display board
- ☐ green, bright green (2), and brown 9" x 12" foam sheets
- ☐ monkey (3), tiger, lion, elephant, alligator, zebra, and grass clump (4) foam stickers
- ☐ two 11" x 2 1/2" pieces of natural-colored burlap or burlap ribbon
- ☐ light blue acrylic paint and paintbrush
- ☐ 5 wood craft sticks
- ☐ tracing paper
- ☐ craft glue
- ☐ craft knife

To make the Theatre:

1. Referring to **Fig. 1**, use the craft knife to cut a 9 1/2" x 6 1/2" opening in the display board center panel.

Fig. 1

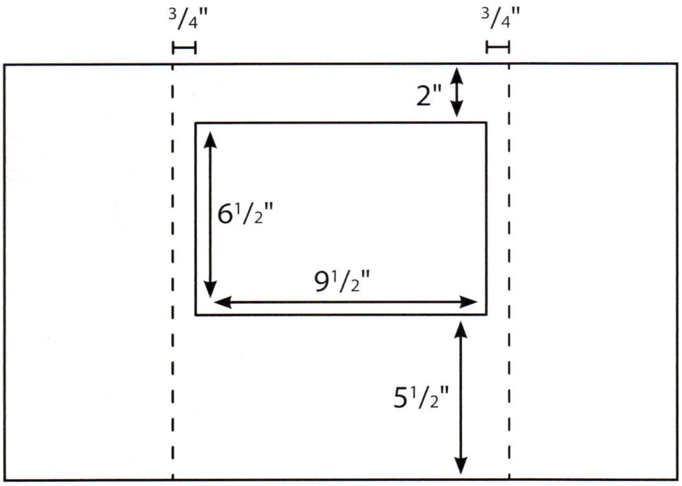

2. Paint the front and back of the display board light blue.

3. Trace the grass, trunk, and tree top patterns (pages 14-15) onto tracing paper. Use the patterns to cut the pieces from the foam sheets.

4. Fringe the bottom 1 1/2" of each burlap piece.

5. Stack and glue the burlap pieces to the top of the display board. Glue the trunks, tree tops, and grass to the display board. Remove the paper backing and add monkeys to the trees, and the alligator and grass clumps to the grass.

To make the Puppets:

Glue each remaining animal sticker to a wood craft stick (do not remove the paper backing).

Play Food

SHOPPING LIST

COOKIES:

- ☐ tan, white, pink, and brown foam sheets
- ☐ colored markers (for "sprinkles")
- ☐ tracing paper
- ☐ craft glue

PIZZA:

- ☐ light red, red, yellow, and tan foam sheets
- ☐ tracing paper
- ☐ craft glue

CHEESEBURGER:

- ☐ red, yellow, orange, bright green, green, brown, and tan foam sheets
- ☐ red and green foam markers
- ☐ decorative-edge scissors
- ☐ tracing paper
- ☐ craft knife
- ☐ craft glue

To make the Cookies:

1. Trace the cookie, frosting, and chip patterns (page 12) onto tracing paper. Use the patterns to cut the pieces from the foam sheets.

2. Glue the chips and frosting to the cookies. Use the markers to add "sprinkles" to the frosting.

To make the Pizza:

1. Trace the pepperoni, cheese, sauce, and crust patterns (page 12) onto tracing paper. Use the patterns to cut the pieces from the foam sheets.

2. Stack and glue the crust pieces together. Glue the sauce, cheese, and pepperoni to the crust.

To make the Cheeseburger:

1. Trace the bun, burger, cheese, lettuce, tomato, pickle, ketchup, and mustard patterns (page 12) onto tracing paper. Use the patterns to cut the pieces from the foam sheets, cutting the burger with the decorative-edge scissors.

2. For the bun bottom, stack and glue two bun pieces together. For the bun top, stack and glue four bun pieces together. Use the craft knife to bevel the bun top edge. Use a dull pencil to draw "sesame seeds" on the bun top.

3. Use the red marker to draw the details on the tomato pieces. Use the green marker to draw "seeds" on the pickle pieces.

Owl Journal

SHOPPING LIST

- ☐ journal or notebook approximately $6^3/_4$" x $9^1/_2$"
- ☐ tan, brown, white, orange, light blue, and black foam sheets for mosaic shapes (we used sticky-back sheets)
- ☐ light blue and blue foam sheets for background (we used sticky-back sheets)
- ☐ 1" foam alphabet stickers
- ☐ tracing paper
- ☐ craft glue (if not using sticky-back foam)

To make the Journal:

1. Cut a $5^1/_2$" x 8" piece of blue foam and a $5^1/_2$" x 1" piece of light blue foam. Remove the paper backing and stick the foam pieces to the journal (or glue them in place).
2. Trace the owl pattern and detail lines (page 16) onto tracing paper and cut out the body (do not cut along the detail lines). Place the pattern on the journal and use a dull pencil to draw around the pattern and over the detail lines, leaving slight indentions in the background foam.
3. Cut foam shapes (such as squares, rectangles, triangles, etc.) of varying sizes to fill in each section of the body. Cut black foam circles for the eyes.
4. Arrange the foam pieces on the background, trimming to fit the body sections as necessary. Remove the paper backing and stick the foam pieces to the background (or glue them in place).
5. Personalize the journal by adding the letters to the background.

"Paper" Dolls

SHOPPING LIST

- ☐ tan, yellow, pink, red, purple, and blue foam sheets
- ☐ foam shape stickers to embellish clothes (we used flowers and a turtle)
- ☐ acrylic jewels
- ☐ black permanent marker
- ☐ red foam marker
- ☐ light red-colored pencil
- ☐ 5/8" round hook and loop fasteners
- ☐ tracing paper
- ☐ craft knife
- ☐ craft glue

To make the "Paper" Dolls:

1. Trace the patterns (page 13) onto tracing paper and cut out. Use the patterns to cut the pieces from the foam sheets.

2. Use the black marker to draw the eyes, nose, and mouth on each body. Use the light red colored pencil to color in the cheeks.

3. Use the red marker to draw the detail lines on the cap. Use the craft knife to cut the slits in the cap and hair.

4. Add the stickers to the shirt and dress. Glue the jewels to the dress.

5. Glue the hook and loop fasteners to the clothes and bodies so the clothes are removable.

Inch Worm Pencil

SHOPPING LIST

- ☐ foam sheet for body
- ☐ 1/2" diameter pom-pom for head
- ☐ two 1/4" diameter pom-poms for antennae
- ☐ two 6mm wiggle eyes
- ☐ chenille stem for antennae
- ☐ 1/4" hole punch
- ☐ craft glue

To make the Inch Worm:

1. Cut a 1" x 8 3/4" foam strip for the body. For the holes, punch holes in the foam as shown in **Fig. 1**.

Fig. 1

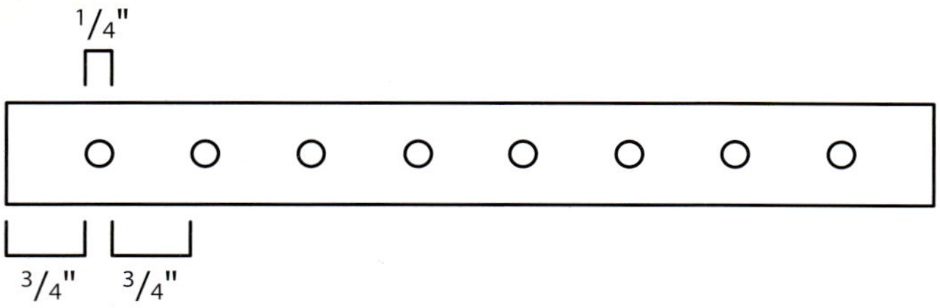

2. For the antennae, cut a 4" chenille stem length. Bend the chenille stem in half and glue a small pom-pom to each end. Glue the antennae to one end of the foam strip.

3. For the head, glue the large pom-pom over the bent part of the antennae. Glue the eyes to the head.

4. When the glue is dry, slide the pencil through the holes, weaving the pencil under and over the foam to create the zigzag body.

Best Friends Puzzle Necklaces

SHOPPING LIST

- ☐ pink foam sheet
- ☐ glittered flower and heart stickers
- ☐ alphabet and heart beads
- ☐ braiding cord
- ☐ large needle
- ☐ tracing paper

To make the Necklaces:

1. Trace the puzzle piece pattern (page 13) and cut out. Use the pattern to cut two puzzle pieces from pink foam.

2. Use the needle to punch a hole on each side of each puzzle piece. Cut two 30" cord lengths.

3. Thread a cord length through a puzzle piece, B, E, S, T, and heart beads, and then back through the puzzle piece. Tie the cord ends together at the desired necklace length. Repeat with the remaining puzzle piece, cord length, and F, R, I, E, N, D, S beads.

4. Add the flower and heart stickers.

Stamps

SHOPPING LIST

- ☐ foam stickers
- ☐ plastic bottle caps

To make the Stamps:

Remove the paper backing from a sticker and stick on a plastic bottle cap. The bottle cap allows you to hold onto the image while stamping.

Mosaic Picture Frame

SHOPPING LIST

- ☐ foam photo frame (ours is about $8^1/_2$" x $6^1/_2$" and holds a 6" x 4" photo)
- ☐ foam sheets for mosaic squares (we used sticky-back sheets)
- ☐ glitter foam star stickers
- ☐ craft glue (if not using sticky-back foam)

To make the Frame:

1. Cut a bunch of foam squares about $^5/_8$" x $^5/_8$". If some are a bit bigger or smaller, it's okay; the size difference creates a more handcrafted look.
2. Arrange the squares on the frame. Remove the paper backing and stick the squares to the frame (or glue them in place). Add the glitter stickers.

Door Hanger

SHOPPING LIST

- ☐ glittered foam door hanger
- ☐ foam alphabet stickers
- ☐ glittered foam shapes stickers

To make the Door Hanger:

Arrange the alphabet and shape stickers on the door hanger. Remove the paper backing and stick on the door hanger.

Wind Sock

SHOPPING LIST

- ☐ light blue 9" x 12" foam sheet
- ☐ foam shape stickers (we used sea-themed stickers)
- ☐ assorted ribbons for hanger and streamers (about $4^{1}/_{2}$ yards total)
- ☐ craft glue

To make the Wind Sock:

1. Roll the light blue foam sheet into a cylinder and glue the short edges together, overlapping the edges by 1".
2. Remove the paper backing and add the foam stickers to the wind sock.
3. For the hanger, cut a 16" ribbon length. Glue the ribbon ends to the inside of the wind sock top on opposite sides.
4. For the streamers, cut about 10 ribbon lengths, varying the lengths from 9" to 14". Glue the streamer ends to the inside of the wind sock bottom.

Visor

SHOPPING LIST

- ☐ glittered foam visor
- ☐ foam sheets for mosaic rectangles (we used 6 colors of sticky-back sheets)
- ☐ craft glue (if not using sticky-back foam)

To make the Visor:

1. Cut foam rectangles of varying sizes.
2. Arrange the rectangles on the visor, trimming to fit the visor shape as necessary. Remove the paper backing and stick the rectangles to the visor (or glue them in place).

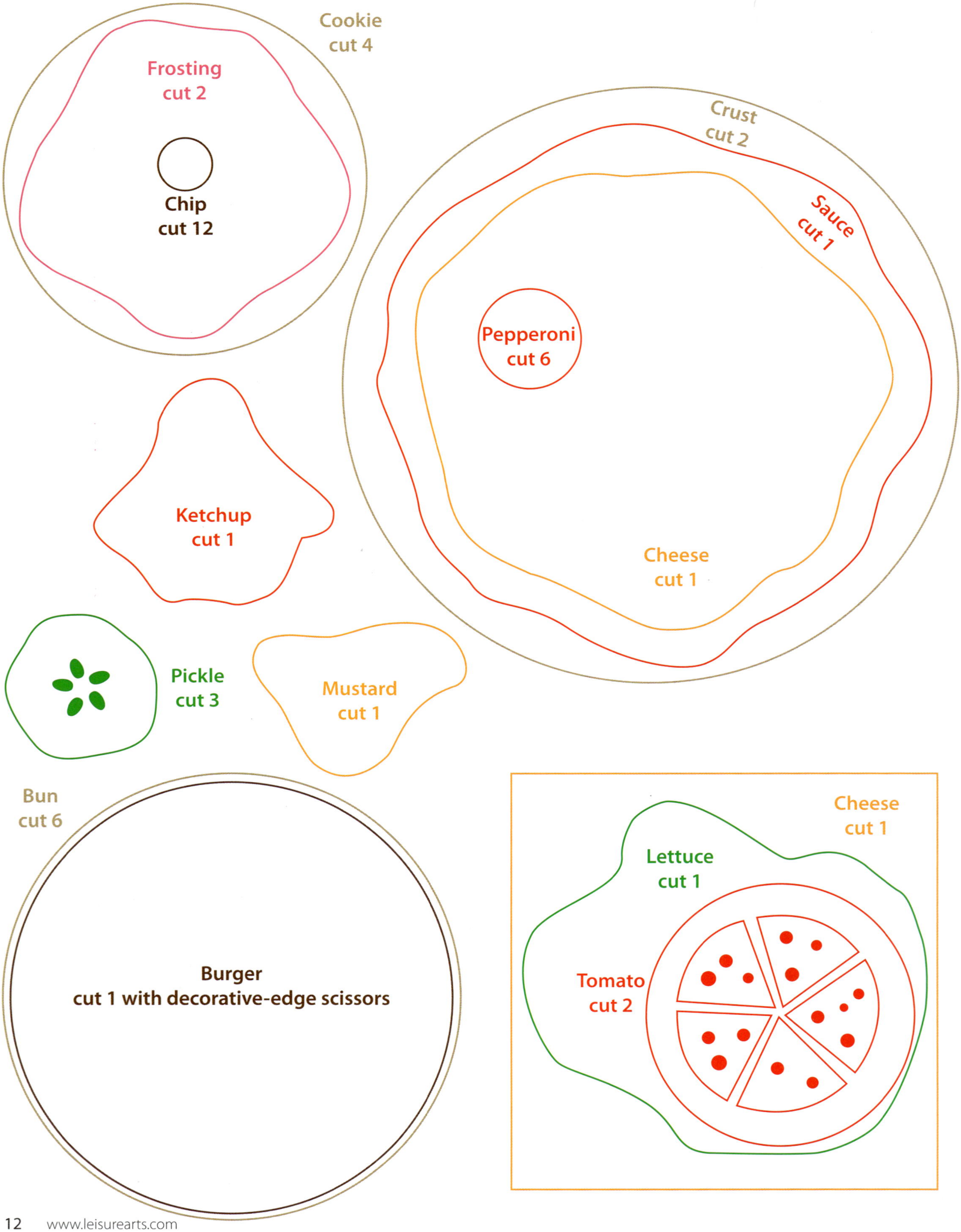
Cookie
cut 4
Frosting
cut 2
Chip
cut 12
Crust
cut 2
Sauce
cut 1
Pepperoni
cut 6
Cheese
cut 1
Ketchup
cut 1
Pickle
cut 3
Mustard
cut 1
Bun
cut 6
Burger
cut 1 with decorative-edge scissors
Cheese
cut 1
Lettuce
cut 1
Tomato
cut 2

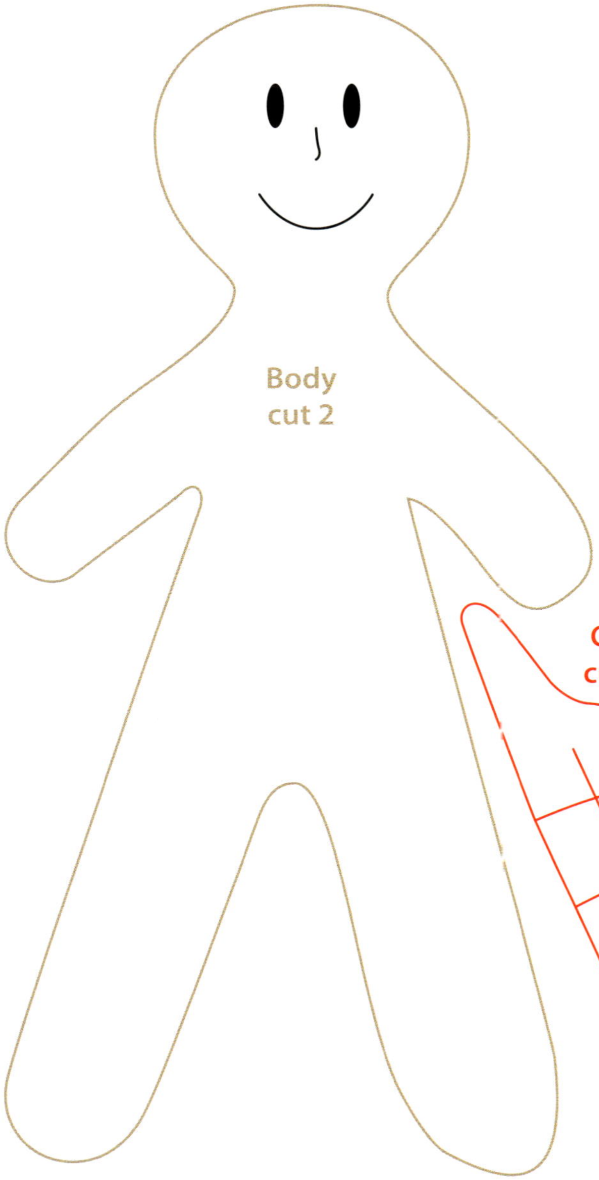
Body
cut 2

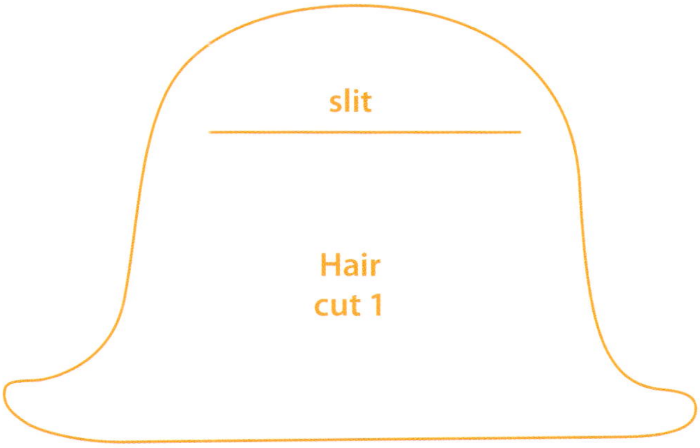
slit
Hair
cut 1

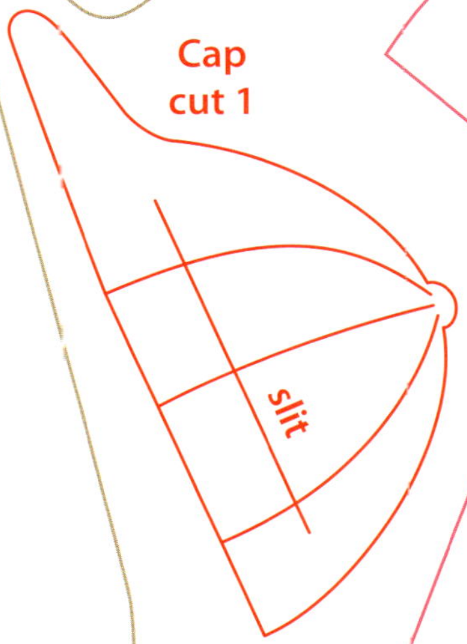
Cap
cut 1
slit

Dress
cut 1

Shirt
cut 1

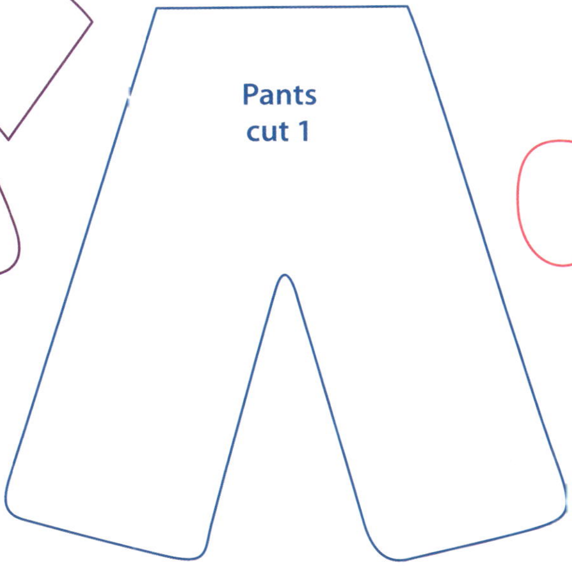
Pants
cut 1

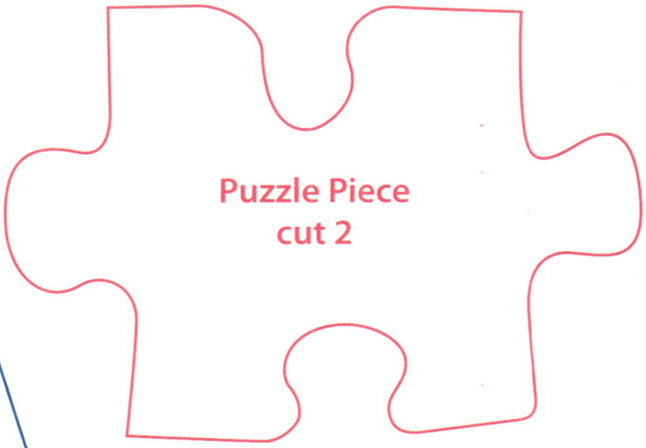
Puzzle Piece
cut 2

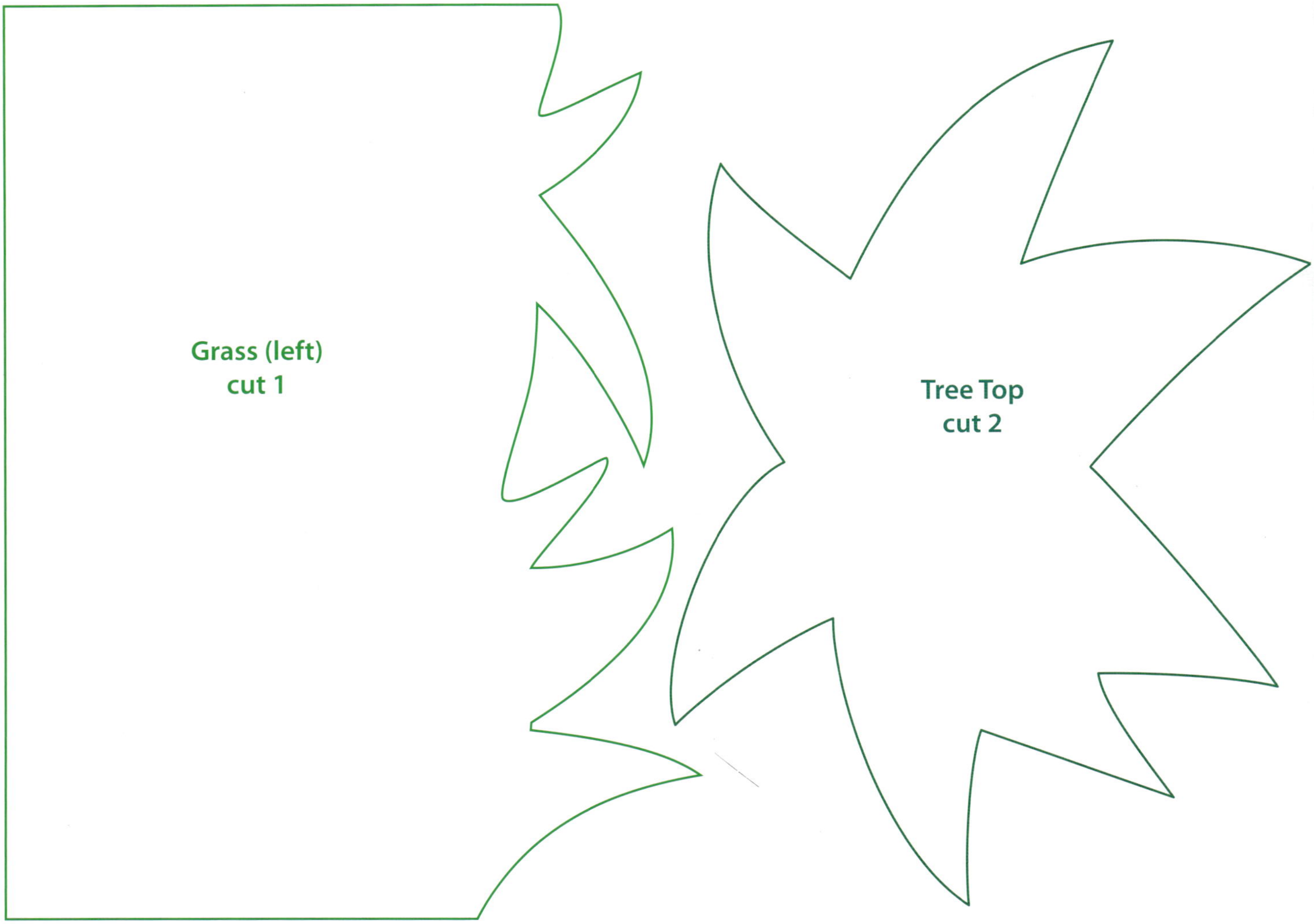
Grass (left)
cut 1
Tree Top
cut 2

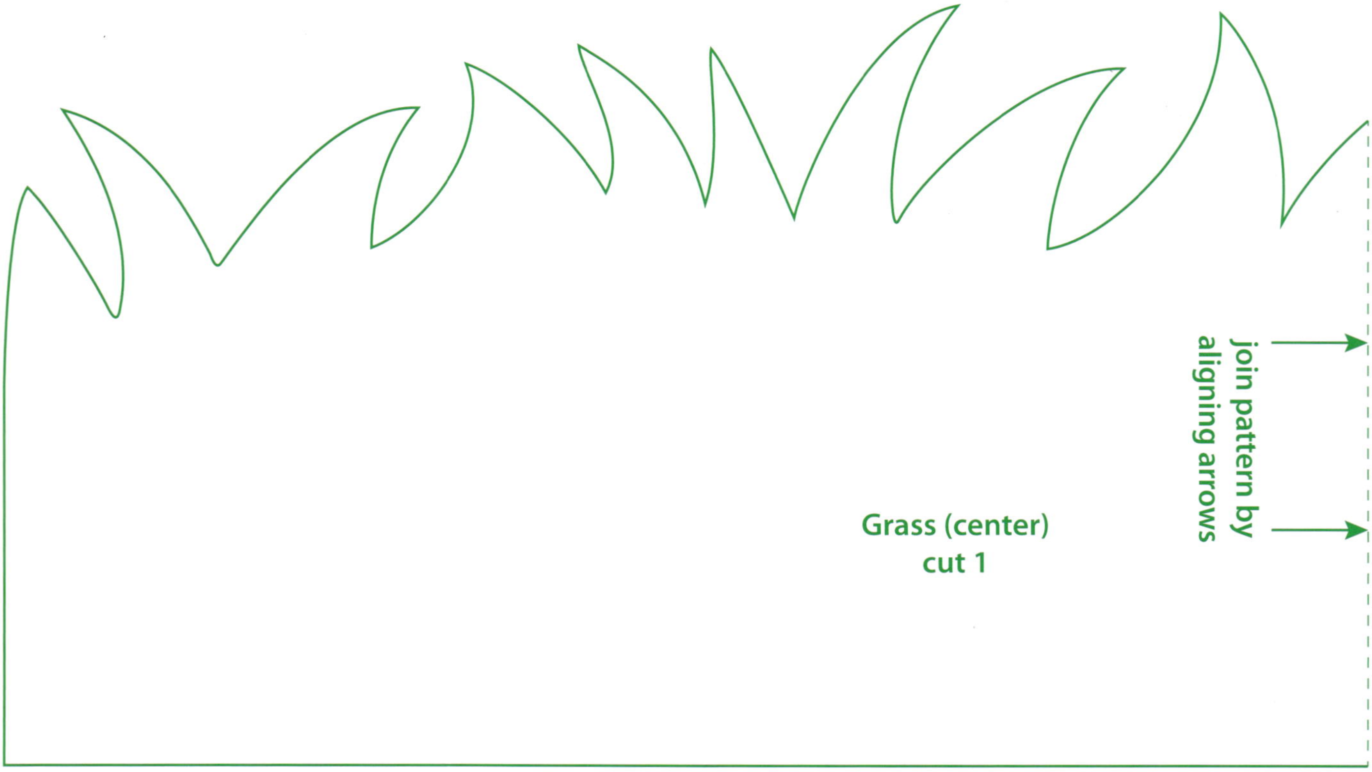
join pattern by
aligning arrows
Grass (center)
cut 1